Gone Forever!
Brachiosaurus

Rupert Matthews

Heinemann Library
Chicago, Illinois

Customer Service 888-454-2279
Visit our website at www.heinemannlibrary.com

Designed by Ron Kamen and Paul Davies and Associates
Illustrations by James Field of Simon Girling and Associates
Photo Research by Rebecca Sodergren and Ginny Stroud-Lewis
Originated by Ambassador Litho Ltd.
Printed and bound in China by South China Printing Company

07 06 05 04
10 9 8 7 6 5 4 3 2

Library of Congress Cataloging-in-Publication Data
Matthews, Rupert.
  Brachiosaurus / Rupert Matthews.
      p. cm. -- (Gone forever!)
Summary: Describes what has been learned about the physical features, behavior, and surroundings of the long-extinct brachiosaurus.
Includes bibliographical references and index.
  ISBN 1-4034-3660-6 (hardcover) -- ISBN 1-4034-3667-3 (pbk.)
  1. Brachiosaurus--Juvenile literature. [1. Brachiosaurus. 2. Dinosaurs.] I. Title.
  QE862.S3M3324 2003
  567.913--dc22
                              2003012295

Acknowledgments
The author and publishers are grateful to the following for permission to reproduce copyright material: pp. 12, 16, 18, 26 AKG; p. 14 Mark Newman/FLPA; p. 20 Museum für Naturkunde, Berlin; pp. 4, 6, 8, 10, 22, 24 Natural History Museum, London. Cover photograph reproduced with permission of Museum für Naturkunde, Berlin.

Special thanks to Dr. Peter Makovicky of the Chicago Field Museum for his review of this book.

Every effort has been made to contact copyright holders of any material reproduced in this book. Any omissions will be rectified in subsequent printings if notice is given to the publisher.

Some words are shown in bold, **like this.** You can find out what they mean by looking in the glossary.

Contents

Gone Forever!

Sometimes all the animals of a certain type die. When this happens, that type of animal has become **extinct**. Scientists called **paleontologists** study extinct animals by digging for **fossils.**

Allosaurus

Brachiosaurus

Kentrosaurus

One extinct animal is Brachiosaurus. This animal was a **dinosaur** that lived about 150 million years ago. Other types of animals lived at the same time as Brachiosaurus. Nearly all the animals that lived then are now extinct.

5

Brachiosaurus's Home

Brachiosaurus **fossils** have been found in rocks. Scientists called **geologists** study these rocks. The rocks can show what the area was like when Brachiosaurus lived there.

Brachiosaurus fossils were found in Africa in 1927.

Brachiosaurus lived in places where the land was flat. There was plenty of water. The weather was warm all year round. Some seasons were wet, and some seasons were dry.

Plants

Scientists have found **fossil** plants in the same rocks as Brachiosaurus fossils. The fossils show them what kinds of plants grew when Brachiosaurus was living. Some of these plants were like those that grow today. Others were very different.

fossil plant leaf

Brachiosaurus lived in open country. Many trees grew in small groups. Some were pine and **fir** trees. They looked a lot like modern trees, but they were much smaller. Some of the plants that lived then are now **extinct.**

Living with Brachiosaurus

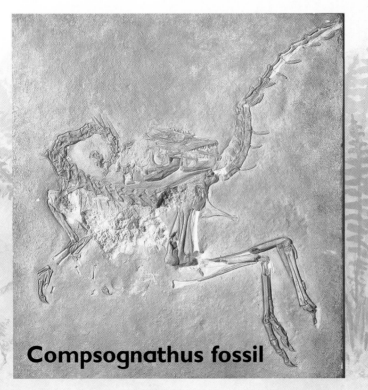

Compsognathus fossil

Paleontologists have also found the **fossils** of beetles and other **insects** in the rocks. This shows that these insects lived at the same time as Brachiosaurus. They also found fossils of small **mammals** that looked like **shrews.**

A tiny **dinosaur** called **Compsognathus** lived among the plants on the forest floor. It hunted mammals, **lizards,** and insects. Compsognathus was about as long as a medium-sized dog. It weighed about the same as a large chicken.

What Was Brachiosaurus?

Paleontologists have studied the **skeletons** of Brachiosauruses. The **fossils** show that Brachiosaurus was a huge animal. It was about as long as five minivans parked end to end!

Brachiosaurus was one of the largest animals ever to live on Earth. Paleontologists believe it walked very slowly. They know that Brachiosaurus ate leaves from trees and other plants.

Growing Up

Paleontologists have found **fossils** of young **dinosaurs** like Brachiosaurus. They believe that Brachiosaurus was probably only about the size of a two-year-old child when it first **hatched.** Perhaps Brachiosauruses hatched from eggs like those shown below.

dinosaur egg fossils

It is possible that young Brachiosauruses hid from meat-eating dinosaurs among the plants on the forest floor. These plants also supplied them with plenty of food. Young Brachiosauruses may also have traveled with a group of grown-up Brachiosauruses as part of a **herd.**

The "Arm Reptile"

The name *Brachiosaurus* means "arm reptile." Scientists gave the **dinosaur** this name because its front legs were longer than its back legs. Most dinosaurs' back legs were longer than their front legs.

Brachiosaurus's long front legs carried the weight of the dinosaur's long neck and head. Powerful shoulder **muscles** kept its head upright. Other muscles moved its legs.

Reaching for Food

Brachiosaurus's neck bones were strong but light. They had large holes in them. This made them less heavy. The bumps on the neck bones were attached to strong **muscles.** The muscles moved the head and neck.

fossil of Brachiosaurus neck bones

Fossil bones show that Brachiosaurus held its neck straight up. This meant it could reach leaves and twigs at the tops of trees. Most **dinosaurs** could not reach this food supply. Brachiosauruses and a few other dinosaurs had it all to themselves.

19

Large Teeth

Brachiosaurus's teeth were large and strong. These teeth were good for stripping tough leaves from plants. Many **fossil** Brachiosaurus teeth are badly worn. This probably means that Brachiosaurus bit through very tough plants.

teeth

Brachiosaurus skull

Brachiosaurus probably ate by snapping its jaws shut on plants and then pulling. It bit off chunks of leaves and twigs and swallowed them whole. Brachiosaurus did not chew its food.

Eating Rocks

Scientists who dig up Brachiosaurus and other **dinosaur fossils** sometimes find piles of rocks nearby. These rocks have been worn smooth. They are called gastroliths, which means "stomach rocks." What were they used for?

Brachiosaurus sometimes swallowed rocks. These rocks stayed in the dinosaur's stomach. They pounded against the leaves eaten by the dinosaur. This helped mash the plants into a soft paste that could be easily **digested.**

23

Danger!

Paleontologists have found **fossils** of a large meat-eating **dinosaur.** This dinosaur is called Allosaurus. Allosaurus lived at the same time as Brachiosaurus. It killed other dinosaurs with its sharp claws and teeth.

sharp teeth

Allosaurus skull

24

Allosaurus could grow as long as a school bus. Scientists think it might have attacked young Brachiosauruses, which were smaller and easier to kill. If several Allosauruses worked together, they might have been able to kill a grown-up Brachiosaurus.

Fighting Back

Brachiosaurus had a large, sharp claw on its front feet. Some **paleontologists** think it used this claw to protect itself from meat-eating dinosaurs. It might also have used it to stop itself from slipping.

claw

Perhaps Brachiosaurus used its large claws to strike
at meat-eaters such as Allosaurus. Or it may have
tried to crush meat-eaters by stomping on them.
Meat-eating dinosaurs usually left larger, older
Brachiosauruses alone.

Where Did Brachiosaurus

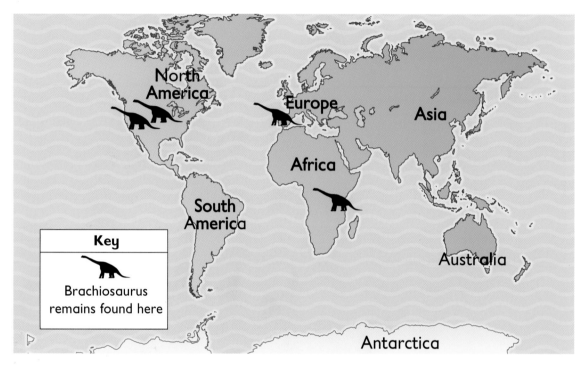

Key

Brachiosaurus remains found here

Fossils of Brachiosaurus have been found in North America, eastern Africa, and western Europe. At the time of Brachiosaurus, these **continents** were joined. There was no Atlantic **Ocean.** The **dinosaurs** could have walked from one continent to the other.

When Did Brachiosaurus Live?

Brachiosaurus lived about 150 to 140 million years ago. It lived in the middle of the Age of the Dinosaurs, which scientists call the Mesozoic Era. Many other large dinosaurs with long necks and long tails lived at about the same time. These dinosaurs are known as **sauropods.**

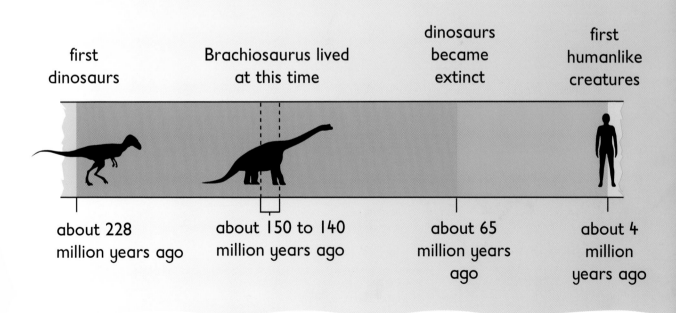

first dinosaurs

Brachiosaurus lived at this time

dinosaurs became extinct

first humanlike creatures

about 228 million years ago

about 150 to 140 million years ago

about 65 million years ago

about 4 million years ago

Fact File

Brachiosaurus	
Length:	up to 92 feet (28 meters)
Height:	up to 46 feet (14 meters)
Weight:	about 66 tons (60 metric tons)
Time:	Late Jurassic Period, about 150 to 140 million years ago
Place:	North America, Africa, Europe

How to Say It

Allosaurus—al-uh-sore-us
Brachiosaurus—brak-ee-os-sore-us
Compsognathus—komp-sog-nay-thuhs
dinosaur—dine-ah-sor
paleontologist—pay-lee-uhn-tahl-uh-jist

Glossary

Compsognathus one of the smallest dinosaurs. It hunted mammals and other small animals.

continent large mass of land, such as Europe or Africa

digested describes the process that happens in the stomach and other body parts so that food can be used by the body for fuel

dinosaur reptile that lived on Earth between 228 and 65 million years ago. Dinosaurs are extinct.

extinct word that describes plants and animals that once lived on Earth but have all died out

fir tree that keeps its leaves all year. The leaves are skinny and always green

fossil remains of a plant or animal, usually found in rocks

geologist scientist who studies rocks

hatch break out of an egg

herd group of animals that lives and travels together

insect small animal with a hard outer covering and six legs

lizard small scaly animal with four legs and usually a long tail

mammal animal with hair or fur. Mammals give birth to live young and feed them on milk from the mother's body.

muscle part of an animal's body that makes it move

ocean very large area of sea

paleontologist scientist who studies fossils to learn about extinct animals, such as dinosaurs

sauropod four-legged dinosaur that ate plants and had a long neck and tail

shrew small mammal with a long nose

skeleton set of bones that holds up the body of an animal

More Books to Read

Cohen, Daniel. *Brachiosaurus*. Mankato, Minn.: Capstone Press, 2003.

Goecke, Michael. *Brachiosaurus*. Mankato, Minn.: Abdo Publishing, 2002.

Wilkes, Angela. *Big Book of Dinosaurs*. New York: Dorling Kindersley, 1994.

Index